SCHIRMER PERFORMANCE EDITIONS

BEETHOVEN

PIANO SONATA NO. 31
IN A-FLAT MAJOR
Opus 110

Edited and Recorded by Robert Taub

Also Available:
BEETHOVEN PIANO SONATAS
edited and recorded by Robert Taub

Volume I, Nos. 1–15
00296632 Book only
00296634 CDs only (5 disc set)

Volume II, Nos. 16–32
00296633 Book only
00296635 CDs only (5 disc set)

On the cover:
The Tree of Crows, 1822 (oil on canvas)
by Caspar David Friedrich
(1774–1840)
© Louvre, Paris, France/Giraudon/The Bridgeman Art Library

ISBN 978-1-4768-1640-1

G. SCHIRMER, Inc.

DISTRIBUTED BY

HAL•LEONARD®
CORPORATION
7777 W. BLUEMOUND RD. P.O. BOX 13819 MILWAUKEE, WI 53213

www.schirmer.com
www.halleonard.com

CONTENTS

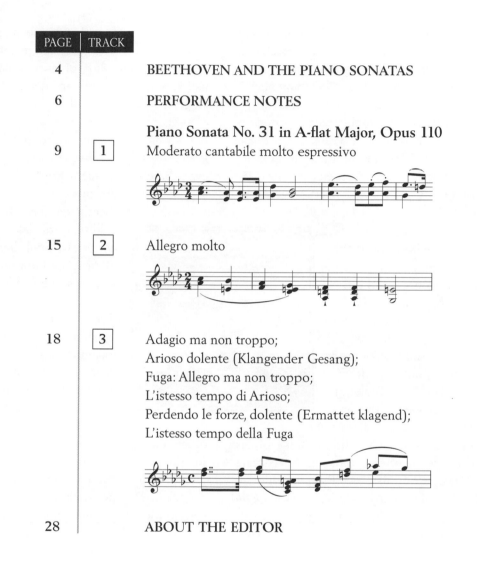

BEETHOVEN
AND THE PIANO SONATAS

In 1816, Beethoven wrote to his friend and admirer Carl Czerny: "You must forgive a composer who would rather hear his work just as he had written it, however beautifully you played it otherwise." Having lost patience with Czerny's excessive interpolations in the piano part of a performance of Beethoven's *Quintet for Piano and Winds*, Op. 16, Beethoven also addressed the envelope sarcastically to "Herr von Zerni, celebrated virtuoso." On all levels, Beethoven meant what he wrote.

As a composer who bridged the gulf between court and private patronage on one hand (the world of Bach, Handel, Haydn, and Mozart) and on the other hand earning a living based substantially on sales of printed works and/or public performances (the world of Brahms), Beethoven was one of the first composers to become almost  obsessively concerned with the accuracy of his published scores. He often bemoaned the seeming unending streams of mistakes. "Fehler—fehler!—Sie sind selbst ein einziger Fehler" ("Mistakes—mistakes!—You yourselves are a unique mistake") he wrote to the august publishing firm of Breitkopf und Härtel in 1811.

It is not surprising, therefore, that toward the end of his life Beethoven twice (1822 and again in 1825) begged his publishers C.F. Peters and Schott to bring out a comprehensive complete edition of his works over which Beethoven himself would have editorial control, and would thus be able to ensure accuracy in all dimensions—notes, pedaling and fingering, expressive notations (dynamics, slurs), and articulations, and even movement headings. This never happened.

Beethoven was also obsessive about his musical sketches that he kept with him throughout his mature life. Desk sketchbooks, pocket sketchbooks: thousands of pages reveal his innermost compositional musings, his labored processes of

creativity, the ideas that he abandoned, and the many others—often jumbled together—that he crafted through dint of extraordinary determination, single-minded purpose, and the inspiration of genius into works that endure all exigencies of time and place. In the autograph scores that Beethoven then sent on to publishers, further layers of the creative processes abound. But even these scores might not be the final word in a particular work; there are instances in which Beethoven made textual changes, additions, or deletions by way of letters to publishers, corrections to proofs, and/or post-publication changes to first editions.

We can appreciate the unique qualities of the Beethoven piano sonatas on many different levels. Beethoven's own relationship with these works was fundamentally different from his relationship to his works of other genres. The early sonatas served as vehicles for the young Beethoven as both composer and pianist forging his path in Vienna, the musical capital of Europe at that time. Throughout his compositional lifetime, even when he no longer performed publicly as a pianist, Beethoven used his thirty-two piano sonatas as crucibles for all manner of musical ideas, many of which he later re-crafted—often in a distilled or more rarefied manner—in the sixteen string quartets and the nine symphonies.

The pianoforte was evolving at an enormous rate during the last years of the eighteenth century extending through the first several decades of the nineteenth. As a leading pianist and musical figure of his day, Beethoven was in the vanguard of this technological development. He was not content to confine his often explosive playing to the smaller sonorous capabilities of the instruments he had on hand; similarly, his compositions demanded more from the pianofortes of the day—greater depth of sonority, more subtle levels of keyboard finesse and control, and increased registral range.

These sonatas themselves pushed forward further development and technical innovation from the piano manufacturers.

Motivating many of the sonatas are elements of extraordinary—even revolutionary—musical experimentation extending into domains of form, harmonic development, use of the instrument, and demands placed upon the performer, the piano, and the audience. However, the evolution of these works is not a simple straight line.

I believe that the usual chronological groupings of "early," "middle," and "late" are too superficial for Beethoven's piano sonatas. Since he composed more piano sonatas than substantial works of any other single genre (except songs) and the period of composition of the piano sonatas extends virtually throughout Beethoven's entire creative life, I prefer chronological groupings derived from more specific biographical and stylistic considerations. I delve into greater depth on this and other aspects of the sonatas in my book *Playing the Beethoven Piano Sonatas* (Amadeus Press).

1795–1800: Sonatas Op. 2 no. 1, Op. 2 no. 2, Op. 2 no. 3, Op. 7, Op. 10 no. 1, Op. 10 no. 2, Op. 10 no. 3, Op. 13, Op. 14 no. 1, Op. 14 no. 2, Op. 22, Op. 49 no. 1, Op. 49 no. 2

1800–1802: Sonatas Op. 26, Op. 27 no. 1, Op. 27 no. 2, Op. 28, Op. 31 no. 1, Op. 31 no. 2, Op. 31 no. 3

1804: Sonatas Op. 53, Op. 54, Op. 57

1809: Sonatas Op. 78, Op. 79, Op. 81a

1816–1822: Sonatas Op. 90, Op. 101, Op. 106, Op. 109, Op. 110, Op. 111

From 1804 (post-Heiligenstadt) forward, there were no more multiple sonata opus numbers; each work was assigned its own opus. Beethoven no longer played in public, and his relationship with the sonatas changed subtly.

—*Robert Taub*

PERFORMANCE NOTES

Extracted from *Beethoven: Piano Sonatas Volume II*, edited by Robert Taub.

For the preparation of this edition, I have consulted autograph scores, first editions, and sketchbooks whenever possible. (Complete autograph scores of only twelve of the piano sonatas—plus the autograph of only the first movement of Sonata Op. 81a—have survived.) I have also read Beethoven's letters with particular attention to his many remarks concerning performances of his day and the lists of specific changes/corrections that he sent to publishers. We all know—as did Beethoven—that musical notation is imperfect, but it is the closest representation we have to the artistic ideal of a composer. We strive to represent that ideal as thoroughly and accurately as possible.

Tempo

My recordings of these sonatas are available as companions to the two published volumes. I have also included my suggestions for tempo (metronome markings) for each sonata, at the beginning of each movement.

Fingering

I have included Beethoven's own fingering suggestions. His fingerings—intended not only for himself (in earlier sonatas) but primarily for successive generations of pianists—often reveal intensely musical intentions in their shaping of musical contour and molding of the hands to create specific musical textures. I have added my own fingering suggestions, all of which are aimed at creating meaningful musical constructs. As a general guide, I believe in minimizing hand motions as much as possible, and therefore many of my fingering suggestions are based on the pianist's hands proceeding in a straight line as long as musically viable and physically practicable. I also believe that the pianist can develop senses of tactile feeling for specific musical patterns.

Pedaling

I have also included Beethoven's pedal markings in this edition. These indications are integral parts of the musical fabric. However, since most often no pedal indication is offered, whenever necessary one should use the right pedal—sparingly and subtly—to help achieve legato playing as well as to enhance sonorities.

Ornamentation

My suggestions regarding ornamental turns concern the notion of keeping the contour smooth while providing an expressive musical gesture with an increased sense of forward direction. The actual starting note of a turn depends on the specific context: if it is preceded by the same note (as in Sonata Op. 10 no. 2, second movement, m. 42), then I would suggest that the turn is four notes, starting on the upper neighbor: upper neighbor, main note, lower neighbor, main note.

Sonata in F Major, Opus 10 no. 2:
second movement, m. 42, r.h.

However, if the turn is preceded by another note (as in Sonata Op. 10 no. 2, first movement, m. 38), then the turn could be five notes in total, starting on the main note: main note, upper neighbor, main note, lower neighbor, main note.

Sonata in F Major, Opus 10 no. 2:
first movement, m. 38, r.h.

Whenever Beethoven included an afterbeat (Nachschlag) for a trill, I have included it as well. When he did not, I have not added any.

Footnotes

Footnotes within the musical score offer contextual explanations and alternatives based on earlier representations of the music (first editions, autograph scores) that Beethoven had seen and corrected. In areas where specific markings are visible only in the autograph score, I explain the reasons and context for my choices of musical representation. Other footnotes are intended to clarify ways of playing specific ornaments.

Notes on the Sonata[1]

PIANO SONATA NO. 31 IN A-FLAT MAJOR, OPUS 110 (1821)

As I begin to play Op. 110, I am careful not to treat the first four measures of the **Moderato cantabile molto espressivo** as an introduction. They are in the moderato tempo—a stately three beats per measure—of the movement, not slower, and I voice the first two measures only slightly to the top. With the *piano subito* and fermata in m. 4, the pulse is flexible. I begin the D-flat trill (m. 4) with a pace that grows out of the sixteenth note that preceded it, increase the speed of the trill with the crescendo, and decrease it only slightly with the decrescendo for a smooth transition to the thirty-second notes that follow.

As the freer cadence in m. 4 leads to an intensely lyrical line over a gentle accompaniment (beginning in m. 5), the qualities of touch change with the right hand really singing out and the left becoming considerably quieter. The area around m. 12 demands an even, light touch, with very slight accentuations on the right-hand notes that Beethoven marked staccato. I make sure not to rush here, and I change the pedal frequently.

The concise development concentrates solely on modulating the harmonic context of the opening motive. Here, for the first time, harmonic motion is intensified, and the opening motive assumes subtly different shadings of mood. Beethoven's legato and dynamic markings are specific for each hand. With the emergence of the theme in a new key (D-flat major) but within the same registral area as m. 5, Beethoven added simply *dolce*. I drop down in dynamic level and play with a very lyrical tone, but maintain the tempo. The place to expand the pulse slightly is at the end of m. 66, as the D-flat prepares to be transformed enharmonically to C-sharp in m. 67.

The scalar second theme is in a lower register of the piano when it recurs in the recapitulation. In the coda, don't rush the first chord of each two-note group, but rather allow it to melt into the resolution. The last two chords of the movement

are strictly in tempo, as are the quarter rests at the end of m. 116, and lead without pause into the Allegro molto.

Although the first movement concludes with rests, the pace continues uninterruptedly, with the first chord of the **Allegro molto** coming where the downbeat of the next measure would ordinarily be. Among the more immediate pianistic challenges of the Allegro molto is that of producing sharp, staccato chords with the right hand in m. 6 while maintaining a legato line with the left-hand octaves. Using pedal would lessen the staccato qualities in the right hand. The tempo is quick (but with a quarter-note pulse, not a half-note pulse) so that the change of fingering on the E octave has to be fast indeed. The two measures of rest (mm. 37–38) provide important drama and cannot be rushed. In the boisterous trio that follows, I use Beethoven's suggested fingering in m. 71.

Although the first three measures of the **Adagio ma non troppo** are of a single tempo, the music becomes highly improvisatory in m.4. Over the next four measures, there are six indicated changes of pacing. The long, unending songful melody begun in m.9 is among the most plaintive, beautifully lyrical lines in the literature. In the spirit of Arioso dolente and Klagender Gesang, the singing right hand floats above the left, although clear articulation of the subtle changes and the left hand's metrical insistence are integral to its mournful nature.

I begin the fugue subject that follows in an almost improvisatory manner. Although the tempo is strict, the sound quality is soft and gentle, as if the theme is being coaxed from the piano. I maintain a pulse of six beats per bar and keep the tempo (Allegro ma non troppo) steady throughout. The bass entrance of the theme in m. 73 three beats early is a jarring surprise, particularly with the *fortissimo*, but I do drop slightly in dynamic level in order to rise again as the ascent of the interval of the fourth continues into m. 80.

Among the most moving features of the second arioso is the way that the line breaks off in mid-phrase—as if quite literally breathing (or sobbing) quietly but passionately—the musical result of thirty-second-rests Beethoven introduced within the line (beginning in m. 120).

1 Excerpted from *Playing the Beethoven Piano Sonatas* by Robert Taub
edited and abridged by Susanne Sheston
© 2002 by Robert Taub
Published by Amadeus Press
Used by permission.

In the midst of the return of the inverted fugal subject, Beethoven places a double augmentation of the subject in counterpoint against a triple diminution: beginning in m. 152 the music is simultaneously twice as slow (top of the right hand) and three times as fast (left hand and inside of the right hand). When the fugue subject returns in tempo (m. 174, fourth beat), the texture is no longer strictly contrapuntal. I maintain the same tempo. The dynamic level is only *forte*; *fortissimo* is reserved for the final cadence. When the fugue subject becomes purely melodic (sforzando, m. 188) in this powerful ending of Sonata Op. 110 the affirmation—the journey of motivic, thematic, and emotional transmogrification—is complete.

Sonata in A-flat Major

Ludwig van Beethoven
Opus 110
Composed in 1821

Moderato cantabile molto espressivo (♩ = 63)

31.

a) *p con amabilità (sanft)*

a) The fingering in italics and the pedal markings are Beethoven's.

10

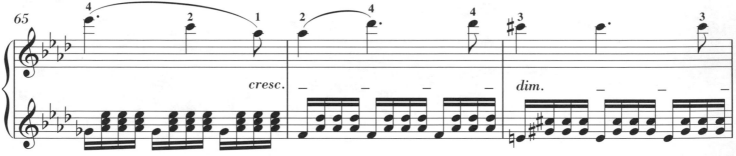

b) In the autograph, this LH slur extends across the bar line (which is at the end of a system), implying extra weightiness. c) This LH slur is present in the autograph, but not in a fair copy (in an unknown hand) owned by Brahms.

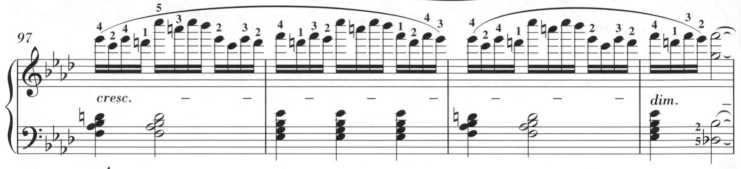

Allegro molto (♩ = 144)

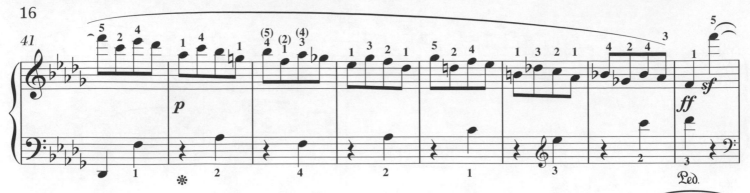

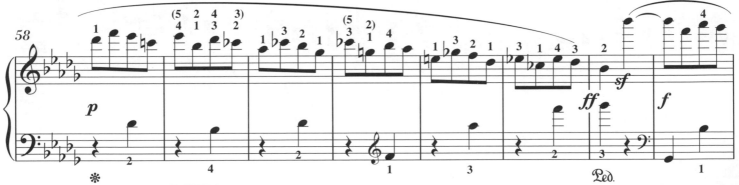

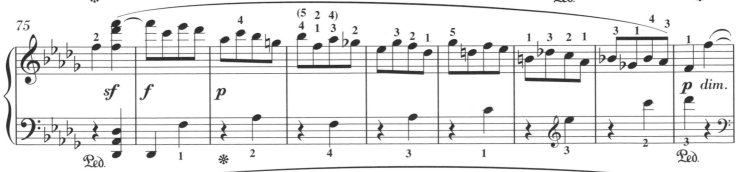

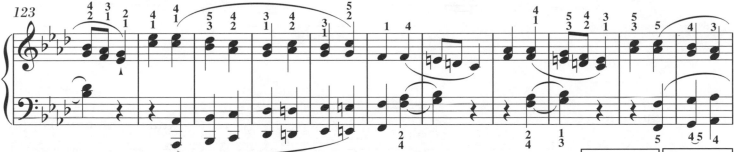

Adagio ma non troppo (♪ = 58)

una corda

4

Recitativo   **più adagio**

andante

cresc.

5

adagio   *ritar - dan - do*   *cantabile*

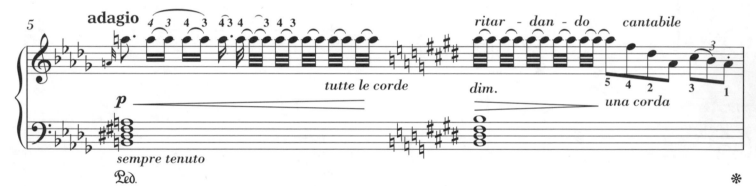

tutte le corde   *dim.*

p   *una corda*

sempre tenuto

6

meno adagio   **adagio**
                              ten.   **Adagio ma non troppo**

cresc.   *dim. smorzando*   *p tutte le corde*

(Klagender Gesang)
Arioso dolente

8

cresc. — — *dim.* *p*

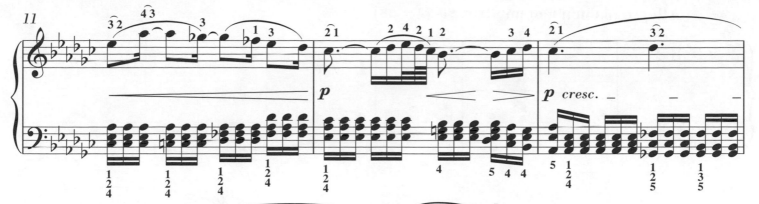

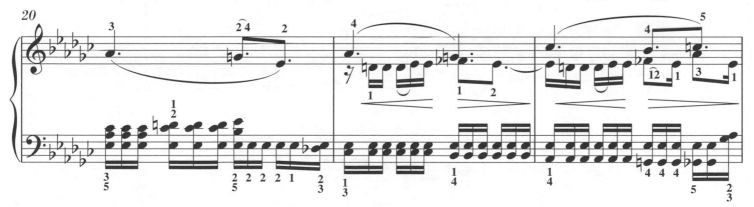

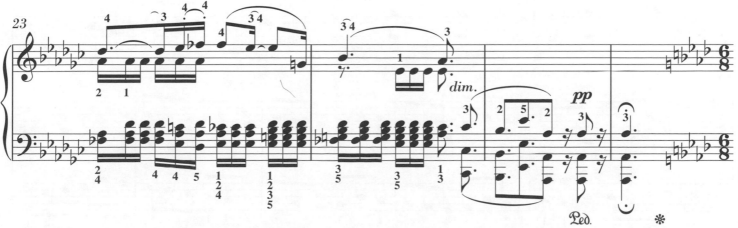

FUGA

Allegro ma non troppo (♩. = 80-84)

L'istesso tempo di Arioso

(Ermattet klagend)
Perdendo le forze, dolente

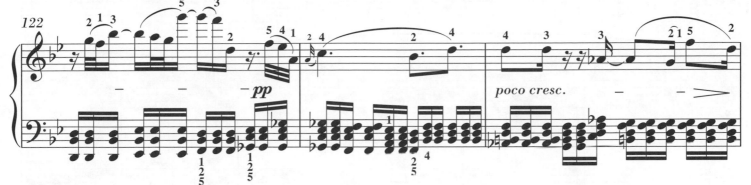

L'istesso tempo della Fuga
poi a poi di nuovo vivente
Nach und nach wieder auflebend

sempre una corda
L'inversione della Fuga (Die Umkehrung der Fuge)

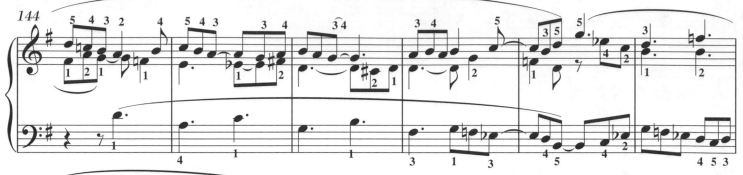

poi a poi tutte le corde

Meno allegro. Etwas langsamer

d) *m.d.*

p

d) As per the autograph score

f) **Tempo primo**

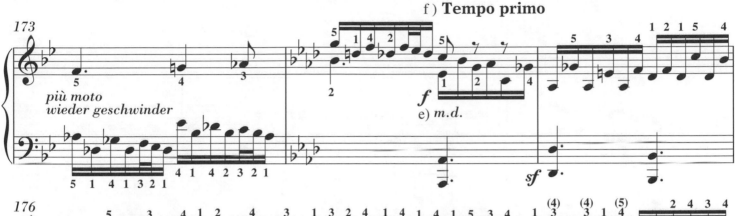

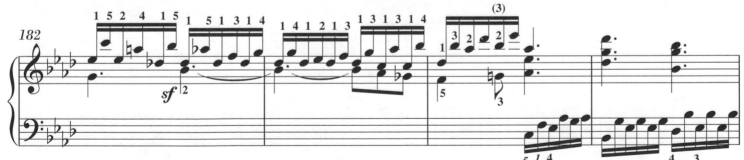

e) As per autograph f) The autograph includes "Tempo primo" on the fourth beat of m. 174, the point at which the Fugue theme returns triumphantly in bass octaves, forte. The acceleration begun with the double diminution in m. 168 culminates at this point. The "Tempo Primo" is not present in the fair copy (unknown hand) in Brahms' possession, nor is it in the first edition. However, there is no evidence that Beethoven deleted—or wished to delete—this marking.

g) E-flat in the autograph, but D-flat in the first edition and the fair copy (unknown hand) owned by Brahms.

ABOUT THE EDITOR

ROBERT TAUB

From New York's Carnegie Hall to Hong Kong's Cultural Centre to Germany's *avant garde* Zentrum für Kunst und Medientechnologie, Robert Taub is acclaimed internationally. He has performed as soloist with the MET Orchestra in Carnegie Hall, the Boston Symphony Orchestra, BBC Philharmonic, The Philadelphia Orchestra, San Francisco Symphony, Los Angeles Philharmonic, Montreal Symphony, Munich Philharmonic, Orchestra of St. Luke's, Hong Kong Philharmonic, Singapore Symphony, and others.

Robert Taub has performed solo recitals on the Great Performers Series at New York's Lincoln Center and other major series worldwide. He has been featured in international festivals, including the Saratoga Festival, the Lichfield Festival in England, San Francisco's Midsummer Mozart Festival, the Geneva International Summer Festival, among others.

Following the conclusion of his highly celebrated New York series of Beethoven Piano Sonatas, Taub completed a sold-out Beethoven cycle in London at Hampton Court Palace. His recordings of the complete Beethoven Piano Sonatas have been praised throughout the world for their insight, freshness, and emotional involvement. In addition to performing, Robert Taub is an eloquent spokesman for music, giving frequent engaging and informal lectures and pre-concert talks. His book on Beethoven—*Playing the Beethoven Piano Sonatas*—has been published internationally by Amadeus Press.

Taub was featured in a recent PBS television program—*Big Ideas*—that highlighted him playing and discussing Beethoven Piano Sonatas. Filmed during his time as Artist-in-Residence at the Institute for Advanced Study, this program has been broadcast throughout the US on PBS affiliates.

Robert Taub's performances are frequently broadcast on radio networks around the world, including the NPR (Performance Today), Ireland's RTE, and Hong Kong's RTHK. He has also recorded the Sonatas of Scriabin and works of Beethoven, Schumann, Liszt, and Babbitt for Harmonia Mundi, several of which have been selected as "critic's favorites" by *Gramophone, Newsweek, The New York Times, The Washington Post, Ovation,* and *Fanfare.*

Robert Taub is involved with contemporary music as well as the established literature, premiering piano concertos by Milton Babbitt (MET Orchestra, James Levine) and Mel Powell (Los Angeles Philharmonic), and making the first recordings of the Persichetti Piano Concerto (Philadelphia Orchestra, Charles Dutoit) and Sessions Piano Concerto. He has premiered six works of Milton Babbitt (solo piano, chamber music, Second Piano Concerto). Taub has also collaborated with several 21st-century composers, including Jonathan Dawe (USA), David Bessell (UK), and Ludger Brümmer (Germany) performing their works in America and Europe.

Taub is a Phi Beta Kappa graduate of Princeton where he was a University Scholar. As a Danforth Fellow he completed his doctoral degree at The Juilliard School where he received the highest award in piano. Taub has served as Artist-in-Residence at Harvard University, at UC Davis, as well as at the Institute for Advanced Study. He has led music forums at Oxford and Cambridge Universities and The Juilliard School. Taub has also been Visiting Professor at Princeton University and at Kingston University (UK).